FABULOUS!

FABULOUS!

THE DAZZLING INTERIORS OF

Tom Britt

by Mitchell Owens

AFTERWORD BY PAIGE RENSE NOLAND

RIZZOLI
NEW YORK

New York · Paris · London · Milan

CONTENTS

PREFACE

Pretty rooms are pretty boring. My preference has always been something totally different: bold, brilliant, even monumental. Rooms you can't forget. Rooms that make you feel important, sexy, confident. Rooms that have a certain swagger. They can have their roots in the court of Louis XV or in the palaces of India, but the point is always the same: to achieve my love for fantasy, always pure and not so simple.

When I was a kid in Kansas City, Missouri, I painted my parents' basement furnace to look like an apple tree in full bloom. Why live with something ugly and utilitarian when you can dress it up and make it memorable? Why be ordinary? You get the picture? I'm always saying to people, "You get the picture?" And I mean it, not as a comic line but as a moment of understanding. I love seeing a client totally get a scheme, when you can see the light come on, when they get as excited as I do about a mirror that literally stretches two stories high or about my plan to punch out a ceiling so their living room flies right up to the roofline and then paint the walls the hottest shade of red you've ever seen—it's all about the gesture. It's all about being unafraid, being fearless.

Ask yourself: Do you really want your house to look like somebody else's? Do you really want to play it safe? I don't think you do. Who would? Why not be fabulous?

Tom Britt
New York, New York

INTRODUCTION

Hearing Tom Britt's voice gives an inkling into his rooms. It is dramatic and resonant, with seemingly every consonant and vowel perfectly and plummily pronounced. It is theatrical and actorly, a Damon Runyon growl with overtones of Jimmy Cagney and Edgar G. Robinson. And like Tom's rooms, it is a voice that rivets.

I moved to Manhattan from Austin, Texas, in 1989, though for some reason I didn't meet Tom until six years later, when I went to see that year's Kips Bay Decorator Show House, which was staged, as it is so very often, in an Upper East Side town house of aristocratic bearing. Tom's voice preceded the room, like a cultured buzz saw. A door opened and there he stood, hair slicked back in French-polish perfection, dressed in a somber, perfectly tailored suit, talking with a woman who seemed utterly rapt by his every forceful syllable. While they chatted, I stood quietly and just absorbed: the vibrant coral-painted walls, a powdery seashell shade with a bit of neon in it; the painted floor patterned with a spreading kaleidoscope of outsize diamonds. Giant gold starburst mirrors hung on the paneled walls, a mid-century Venetian chandelier hovered overhead like an iridescent UFO, and the French-inflected armchairs were dressed in carnation-pink leather, or maybe it was satin. There was blue, and there was yellow, too, elements of what Suzanne Slesin in the *New York Times* called "a frothy extravaganza of high-intensity color combinations."

Formal yet madcap, the living room that Tom had wrought—it was his first Kips Bay space in more than twenty years—was a rapturous space, and, yes, like some of his best décors, it was slightly bonkers. It had bravery and panache and guts. The combination of objects and colors and styles resembled nothing I had ever seen before, and at that moment, I fell in love with Tom's crazy, fabulous world, a universe where style, gossip, and recklessness meet in a kind of circus of chic. That taste—triumphant, daredevil, nose-thumbing, often challenging, always cinematic—is what *Fabulous!* celebrates. Think of it as decoration that is a force of nature, intended to astonish, envelope, and, yes, inspire.

Tom's primary stage for much of his career was *Architectural Digest*, the magazine where the decorator's finest interiors were regularly showcased from the mid 1970s through the early 2000s. Fiercely protective of her turf, longtime editor in chief Paige Rense was a benevolent dictator who kept her preferred designers and architects close and their work even closer. She famously insisted on right of first refusal, and woe betide any talent who attempted to circumvent that unstated rule without her express approval. Says Britt, "You'd have to have been crazy to try that."

The extraordinary archives at Condé Nast, which purchased *Architectural Digest* (now known as *AD*) in 1993, are a rich repository of coast-to-coast Brittiana from Florida bungalows to New York City penthouses to Kansas City mansions to Northern California seaside retreats. Britt's interiors range in style as widely as their geographical locations and as distinctly as their architectural envelopes, so *Fabulous!* loosely gathers them into themes: Exotic, Modern, Historical, and Classic. That being said, the categories are fairly elastic; some entries can be partially in one and partially in another, depending on Britt's inspired juggling and his multiple, sometimes overlapping, frames of aesthetic reference. More so than many designers who are part of the same notably impactful generation that came of age in the 1950s and '60s—among them Mario Buatta, Richard Callahan, Angelo Donghia, Mark Hampton, Bunny Williams, and Edward Zajac—Britt has emphasized artistic breadth over pigeonholing, and his clients have welcomed his preference for experimentation and iconoclasm. Numerous individuals, most of them repeat clients, have given Britt carte blanche with their interiors, which, considering his forceful nature and certainty in his own taste ("You either have it or you don't," he told me) is often the path of least resistance and greatest success.

As Britt matured as a tastemaker and became more of an aesthetic force, his work became stronger, more robust, and, frequently, unabashedly theatrical. Timelessness, though, is subjective. No designer's portfolio can ever guarantee that enviable state, given the variables of taste and budget. But every top-flight interior designer can point to creations that live well beyond the rooms' moment of creation—to spaces that still speak eloquently decades later. The ones that have been selected for inclusion in *Fabulous!* are just that: Britt's most outstanding and transporting environments, thirty-two high-point projects that still look fabulous.

Mitchell Owens

EXOTIC

FANTASIES MADE REAL • THE FARAWAY BROUGHT HOME
OPULENCE WITH AN ATTITUDE

NEW YORK ♦ NEW YORK

2007

Clients who rely on Britt to conjure up one
domestic scenario often come back for more, as a debut
apartment can lead to a country place, a beach house,
a ski lodge, and a pied-à-terre, all bearing the designer's
vivid stamp. And very often that devotion to Britt
environments is inherited by the younger generation
as they grow up and settle into spaces of their own.
Consider, for instance, a young fashion designer
for whom Britt has been a life constant: not only
was the decorator an old friend of her father's
and a groomsman at her parents' wedding, he also
has decorated all but one of the family's numerous
homes, from East Coast to West Coast.

When the designer and her husband,
a real estate developer, acquired a duplex apartment
in a handsome 1902 loft building in Greenwich Village
a little more than a decade ago, the newlyweds left
everything to Britt. After the designer and his associate
Peter Napolitano gutted the apartment and sprinkled
in gutsy classical cornices and mantels, Britt and
another colleague, Valentino Samsonadze, conceived
shimmering, saturated rooms that are perfectly suited
to a young couple appreciative of far-off locales.

Jewel-tone-painted walls and metallic finishes—even some ceilings are silvered—meet animal prints, Ottoman and pan-Asian furnishings, and a sprinkling of deluxe classics. Napoléon III–style rope-twist armchairs, each painted gloss white and upholstered in leopard-spot velvet, add a dash of Second Empire frivolity to the spacious living-dining-kitchen area, where the walls are a brilliant robin's-egg blue and Moroccan polychrome-glass lanterns hang from the silver-papered ceiling. One wall hosts a large photograph of a rampaging African elephant by Peter Beard, which is as thrilling to look at as it was vital to Britt's creative process. The pachyderm's raised trunk led the designer to combine curving Thai architectural fragments into custom-made mirrors to hang above the rooms' white plaster mantels, one of which is flanked by Middle Eastern cabinets that are encrusted with shimmering nacre.

Iridescence gives the home a literally polished look. Silver paint coats contemporary reproductions of eighteenth-century Cockpen chairs, a Scottish variant of Chinese Chippendale. Occasional tables, whether Art Moderne in spirit or Parsons in style, are paved with mirror. One object after the next shimmers and shines, from vintage mixed-metal vessels by Germany's Wurttembergische Metallwarenfabrik (WMF) to rock-crystal candlestick lamps.

The master bedroom takes this shine-on chic to a rapturous extreme. Ceiling and walls are romantically papered in a lacy silver-on-white pattern that replicates traditional Mughal jalis, or lattice panels, like those at the Taj Mahal. The fretwork motif gives the chamber the feeling of a precious birdcage while diminishing the architecture's multitude of corners and angles into insignificance.

LAWRENCE · NEW YORK

1991

The Long Island enclave of Lawrence, a genteel vestige
of pre-Colonial times, is hardly where one expects to
find a house that speaks eloquently of the farthest
reaches of Southeast Asia. But Britt's interiors for the
weekend residence of a globetrotting fashion-world
couple references the clients' business trips to that
humid part of the world, which happens to be one of the
designer's own favorite stomping grounds.

Rather than transform the interiors of the 1890s brick house into a stagey simulacrum of getaways in Bali or Thailand, Britt relied on a suggestive yet simple scheme. Throughout the house, spectacularly overstuffed sofas and chairs are uniformly upholstered in a nubby cream-tone chenille that gives them the spatial presence of snow-covered boulders amid the existing dark paneling and chimneypieces. The seating's irrational proportions are surprisingly seductive but also a bit of visual trickery, causing the rooms to seem more generous in scale, in spite of the relatively low ceilings. Tall potted raffia palms fool the eye as well, while the dramatically beamed ceilings in the living room and dining room seem to turn those spaces into virtual pergolas.

Treasures from the homeowners' travels—gilded Buddhas, Thai artifacts, and the like—are sprinkled amid this interior landscape, rounded out with culturally related objects that Britt found in Asia as well as the United States, such as the eighteenth-century Chinese benches that serve as cocktail tables in the living room. In the dining room, an antique altar table stretches across the wainscot, a fretwork platform for Asian ceramics in electric shades of blue, yellow, and green.

Britt's only significant deviation from the Far East is the master bedroom, where a taste of nineteenth-century Europe prevails. There, a pair of eccentric Viennese beds—pushed together to make one large bed and set importantly within a shallow alcove—and a Charles X pedestal table glow like aged amber amid the pale suede-covered walls.

KANSAS CITY • MISSOURI

1982

One of Kansas City's leading lights, a deft hostess
and a perceptive collector of nineteenth-century mercury
glass, turned to Britt when she, newly divorced,
took a one-bedroom flat at the city's most prestigious
address: the Walnuts, a 1930 Jacobean-style
apartment complex by architects Jesse F. Lauck
and Elmer R. Boillot.

Many of the client's multicultural furnishings, works of art, and decorative objects—notably a very large nineteenth-century Chinese carpet with eloquently faded cream, brown, and coral-pink—had been used in her previous residences. But the Walnuts apartment required a different point of view, soigné but refreshing, a décor that speaks of her decades of connoisseurship and also her new stage in life.

Britt closed the fireplace, removed the mantel, and filled that section of wall with a floor-to-ceiling sheet of mirrored glass to give an illusion of greater space. Set flush with the mirror is a jet-black cocktail table, which is used as a stage for an eighteenth-century Guanyin figure.

Britt's décor sets the client's belongings against dramatically different backgrounds, one for entertaining and one for privacy. The living-dining room is painted a glossy, seductive shade of dark chocolate-brown that brings the sleek sofas upholstered in white Thai silk, the cream-and-giltwood Louis XVI–style chairs, and the Chinese carpet into sharper focus. The smudgy pink of the carpet is deployed as an accent color throughout the space, showing up in the chairs' upholstery and the sweeping curtains, as well as being echoed in a Helen Frankenthaler abstract print and a wall-size Tibetan religious painting.

The bedroom is light, soft, and feminine, in strikingly cozy contrast to the apartment's glamorous main space. A printed Indian cotton, neutral in tone and tightly ruched, lines the walls and curtains the windows. The only splash of color, largely rose-pink and sky-blue, comes from a transporting historical scene that Britt placed opposite the bed so that it would be the first thing seen each morning: a folding screen depicting bewigged courtiers milling before Louis XIV's Grand Trianon beneath a cloud-specked sky.

NEW YORK • NEW YORK

2001

For the 2001 Kips Bay Decorator Show House,
Britt was given one of the event's prime spaces:
the paneled living room of a circa 1915 Park Avenue
town house designed by Manhattan architecture firm
McKenzie, Voorhees & Gmelin. What the designer
turned in is a seductive, fast-forward salon with
an opulent sensibility and cosmopolitan contents.

Spare arrangements of antique and modern treasures
are set amid two-tone periwinkle walls, sumptuous
expanses of amber velvet, and an ebony-dark parquet.
Nineteenth-century Japanese gilded paper screens
depicting the iconic Uji Bridge fan out from a low golden
streamlined sofa that is attended by 1950s
T. H. Robsjohn-Gibbings slipper chairs. The towering
Venetian mirror reflects an even broader span of style:
A Louis XV bracket clock is framed by 1960s Abstract
Expressionist works by Al Held, and, just out of sight,
a vaporous 1970s Kenneth Noland target painting in
color-coordinated tones of blue and yellow is suspended
above an amber-velvet corner banquette. Mod-medieval
sconces and Hansen crystal-rod floor lamps provide
intimate pools of light.

NEW YORK • NEW YORK

2008

Britt's revamp of Doubles, the Social Register luncheon and dinner club located
in the basement of the 1928 Sherry-Netherland Hotel, builds brilliantly on its storied past.
The club, when it opened in 1976, heralded an effulgently streamlined scheme by Valerian Rybar.
Subsequent work was completed by Betty Sherrill of McMillen and, later, by Tom Britt in 1995.
Finally, in the summer of 2008, Britt and his associate Valentino Samsonadze completed
a more major and lasting redecoration, the current seraglio-chic red-and-gold setting.

In the bar area, red walls—glossily lacquered with Venetian plaster— are framed with sparkling brass trim, while matching crocodile hide–stamped leather covers the banquettes. A flowering tree, which seems as much Mughal as it does Jazz Age, flings its painted boughs across gold trompe-l'oeil trelliswork, the latter's crisscrossing echoed in fretwork carpeting. In the Game Room, existing Robert Davison paintings peopled with rajas and ranis inspired Britt to paint the folding doors with an artful evocation of a subcontinental pavilion (overleaf).

For the main dining room, which has been in varying shades of red since its inception and is centered on a small dance floor, Britt advanced the famously hedonist décor devised by Rybar into something fantastic yet respectful, splashing walls with a blossomed textile and installing outrageously exaggerated banquettes. The latter's scrolling and sculpted backs are a dizzy baroque counterpoint to the decades-old chrome dining chairs, which Britt updated with satiny red stripes. The designer also applied mirrored glass details to the flowered walls, reflective bands that stretch up and join the 1970s metallic cornice in a bravura gesture that tangibly and spiritually connects Britt's vision with the glamour that came before.

NAPLES ⋅ FLORIDA

1990

The relative modesty of a couple's Gulf Coast residence, which Britt first decorated in the 1970s
shortly after the clients wed (see pages 90–97), had become grand and fantastically madcap by the 1990s,
a fitting home for a dynamic husband and wife and their three popular daughters.
A building that had been constructed in a denatured Georgian Revival style morphed into a wildly pretty
British Colonial extravaganza, thanks to Britt and society architect Kasimir Korybut-Daszkiewicz.
The interiors combine powerhouse glamour and cheeky folderol. Freestanding fluted columns
topped with potted plants march down the mirrored entrance gallery.

For the enormous living room, which combines two earlier spaces, Britt brought in plump quilted sofas with massive rolled arms and chubby slipper chairs covered in a silver-and-gray awning stripe.

Joining the living room's capacious seating are white, gold, and silver antiques, most glamorously a couple of sets of Venetian grotto furniture, some of which stand in the trellised dining room that was retained from Britt's 1970s scheme. The designer acquired an array of gilded nineteenth-century Old Paris porcelain fruit baskets and used them as gleaming cachepots for shocking-pink New Guinea impatiens and magenta orchids.

The private rooms are as rambunctious as the shared spaces. In the library, Britt offhandedly paired a brash plaid with a white cotton patterned with trailing water lilies. On tables and the mantel he deployed more than a dozen glass candlesticks in a milky shade of breath-mint blue.

The master bedroom is like a veranda from a play set in the Deep South in Victorian times. The sole fabric—used for the cushions, the upholstery, and even the underside of the bed's canopy—is a pink-printed moiré splashed with violets and geraniums, dressing a room that is densely furnished with white-painted vintage wicker tables, chairs, and planters subsumed by a tropical jungle of Phalaenopsis orchids, African violets, impatiens, and potted palms.

NEW YORK • NEW YORK

2004

Fantasies often are best when rendered suggestively rather than literally.
Britt's dining room in New York City's Time Warner Center—part of a 2004 *Architectural Digest*–
sponsored design showcase staged at the new condominium building—is an atmospheric lesson,
paring exoticism to an eloquent minimum while blending enough styles and cultures
to encourage individual flights of fancy.

With a Kenneth Noland target painting acting as an otherworldly sun,
the silver-walled space is furnished with Britt's favorite Directoire-style side chairs,
a model that he adapted from an early nineteenth-century original that he has long admired.
These elegant seats surround silvery pedestal tables that he designed
and which rest in the virtual shade cast by an English Regency metal palm tree.

It is a setting that conjures up a multitude of mental images, largely of swish French colonials abroad,
from Napoléon Bonaparte's beautiful sister Pauline and her eventful sojourn in Haiti to—
thanks to the presence of an antique Buddha, sublimely supine—Parisian expats living it up in Annam
in the 1920s. One would not be in the least surprised to see a monkey burst in from the jungle that must
surely be just out of view, or to see squawking parrots flutter in and preen themselves
on the tree's golden fronds as Noland's sun shines eternally on.

SAN FRANCISCO • CALIFORNIA

2014

Given the clients' lifelong affection for Paris,
it stands to reason that Britt afforded one of their
numerous residences a strong Gallic accent.
This flat, a San Francisco pied-à-terre, seems straight
out of the pages of Marcel Proust's *In Search of Lost
Time*, perhaps as a setting for Odette de Crécy, the
demimondaine who eventually made good and gained
a couple of august titles on her social ascent.

Britt's operatic décor is at once sexy, luxurious, and powerful, from the gold-leafed ceilings to the glossy scarlet walls to the leopard-spot carpeting (and matching cushions) that knits the main rooms together. Dripping with long tassels, a pair of button-tufted low chairs known as chauffeuses join Louis XVI bergères and brilliantly gilded console tables, again in the Louis XVI style. It's a sumptuous vocabulary that would not look out of place at, say, the Tuileries Palace during the Second Empire.

The palette is rapturous and daring: the red walls are balanced with silk fabrics in equally strong shades of yellow, blue, and pink, the solid blocks of color packing a greater punch than any print could. But Britt deftly cools down the heated polychromy with doses of black and white, including diamond-pattern floors and awning stripes that crown the windows and transform the glass-walled dining area into a romantic tented pavilion.

Red fades to candy pink in the master
bedroom, though the complementary accents—
leopard-spot carpeting and a glamorous
gold-leaf ceiling—remain the same.

MODERN

CLARITY AND CRISPNESS · THE SHOCK OF THE NOW
SIMPLY SENSATIONAL

NEW YORK • NEW YORK

2008

Architectural envelopes that soar and spread are particularly well suited to Britt's aesthetic swagger.
That kind of square footage allows for exclamatory flamboyance: succulent colors, curtains that
cascade like waterfalls from impossible heights, powerful patterns that seem to repeat into infinity,
and gutsy works of art as big as billboards. A strikingly glamorous home in New York City's
Tribeca neighborhood offers such a decorative case study. Completed in 2002 by John Petrarca
of Guenther Petrarca, an architecture firm celebrated for creating Lower Manhattan residences
that evoked the area's industrial and mercantile past, the slender five-story building barely attracts
the eye. Its warm redbrick details and overscale, painted steel windows blend discreetly into
a streetscape composed of nineteenth- and early twentieth-century loft buildings.

After the town house was purchased by young art collectors with roots in South Asia
and a toddler son, Britt and associate Valentino Samsonadze were called in to make magic.
The brand-new spaces that confronted them were high, white, and clinically spare,
and every corner of the five-bedroom address was entirely free of conventional diversions
such as cornices and moldings. Another designer might have proposed a dramatic
and expensive remodel or suggested the installation of ennobling details to counteract the interiors'
operating-room atmosphere. Britt, however, chose to keep his work simple, telling the clients
that he wanted to bring "glamour and warmth to an austere building."

The designer's recipe is equal parts caffeinated punches of color and a theatrical sense of scale. A bold four-color palette—creamy white punctuated by coral, black, and a shade of red as brilliant as the traditional bindi that dots the foreheads of Hindu women in Britt's beloved India—sets the tone for the spirited public spaces. Glossy coral walls in the street-level entrance hall give way to white and red when the open staircase ascends to the second floor, which Britt humorously calls "the piano nobile." This level is largely given over to living and dining areas furnished with plump, streamlined upholstery and is tied together with red-and-white diamond-pattern carpets.

The piano nobile's pièce de résistance is Britt's treatment of the double-height wall of glass that dominates the rear of the living area. Measuring twenty-two feet long, white drapes extend down from the high ceiling and are tied back to frame the terrace beyond. The majestic snowy swags and fantastical valance, trimmed with a wide band of scarlet, make an audacious impact that recalls Hollywood set decoration—think *Gilda* with Rita Hayworth or any musical concocted by Busby Berkeley—where chic begins to shade into camp. It is a characteristic bravura, double-dare gesture from Britt, a man who is as much an impresario as he is a decorator. Even the terrace, planted with red-leaf begonia and coleus, adheres to his prescribed palette.

The bedrooms, on the other hand, turn down the chromatic temperature with cool blues, silver-leaf walls, shimmering silks, and Britt's hallmark Indian-style low tables inlaid with mother-of-pearl. Still, there's drama, though in a smaller but still heady dose. Another great sweep of parted curtains, this time sapphire blue lined with saffron yellow, frame the guest room's divan, creating an alcove that puts the room's occupants on display as much as it focuses all eyes on the bed where they slumber (overleaf). And, as was his want, Britt made unexpected and memorable marriages of styles and materials, in this space combining straight-laced Louis XVI–style commodes with an earthy, antique, and zigzag-motif dhurrie.

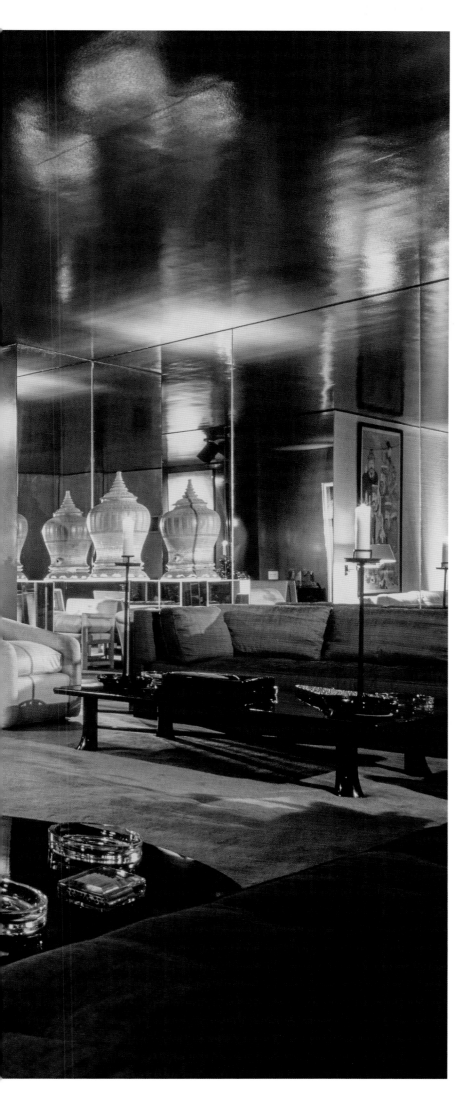

NEW YORK • NEW YORK

1980

Mirror can be the salvation of many a small space.
A wall of mirror at one end of a living room can make
it appear twice as long, and a thorough layering of
reflective glass on walls, ceiling, and cabinets can make
a meager bath feel as expansive as a spa. But there is much
more to establishing a feeling of spaciousness,
even grandeur, within challenged square footage.

Highly social clients from Mexico City contacted Britt after acquiring a one-bedroom pied-à-terre in Olympic Tower, the midtown Manhattan skyscraper designed by Skidmore, Owings & Merrill. They intended to use the space frequently for entertaining, from intimate drinks parties to lively late-night dinners. Spatial limitations were great; the apartment is replete with relatively low ceilings and a central L-shape space that accommodates areas for both living and dining. Beyond that, the envelope, banal in detail and basic in execution, offers no transcendent moments in terms of fine architecture—though a tall, wide window frames a cinematic view of the palatial Plaza Hotel, leafy Central Park, and the glittering skyscrapers of midtown Manhattan.

Britt's approach was twofold and inspiringly successful. The living and dining room are treated as a single, seamless space. Each area remains true to its individual purpose, but they are chromatically linked through a calm and embracing palette of chocolate brown and off-white, featured in decorative elements from the upholstery to the carpeting. Plainly tailored but lusciously upholstered furniture underscores the apartment's easy elegance, such as the solid, simple dining chairs, Britt standards that could be described as the Parsons table of seat furniture for the designs' ability to maintain their integrity no matter the fabric that covers them.

Reflectivity—here direct, there subtle— is paramount to the apartment's makeover. The ceiling is quietly glossy, coated with an iridescent pale nougat. One dining-area wall is clad in brown Siamese silk, while a living-area wall wears a white version of the same textile. Other walls are sheathed with silvery mirror, strategically installed so that each space can be partially viewed from the other. Thus, the earthy colors meld and repeat and reflect into infinity, and the room's small footprint seems greatly expanded, all without moving a single wall. Low furniture plays an important spatial role, too, its stature causing the ceiling heights to seem more generous.

Asian accents underscore Britt's calming and uniform palette while also, through their coloration, complementing it. The reds and oranges seen in the apartment's reproduction Qing-dynasty paintings are echoed throughout the rooms—in Thai covered jars placed on mirrored pedestals, in a Japanese box shaped like a fish, and in an eloquent statue of Guanyin that overlooks the bedroom. Doses of contemporary culture, including a Gene Davis lithograph of colorful parallel stripes, lend rigor and dash, as do low Chinese-style tables finished with gleaming black lacquer.

A few years after the project was completed, Britt's clients asked him to come back and refresh the rooms. This time around, rather than a wholesale redecoration, the designer focused largely on recoloring, eliminating the calming neutrals and adopting energetic reds.

NAPLES·FLORIDA

1976

Flexibility in decoration can mean the ability to create
interiors with multiple purposes or to juggle style-spanning
furniture and art into a welcoming coherence. For Britt,
it also means the ability to take a décor that was planned
for a far more formal address—in this case a glamorous prewar
Manhattan apartment—and transfer it to and adapt
it for a polar-opposite destination: a mid-century English
Georgian-inspired house on Florida's Gulf Coast,
where cool terrazzo takes the place of warm parquet.

Shortly after their 1969 wedding, a couple, who would become lifelong Britt clients, suddenly decided to leave behind New York City for Naples, Florida. Accompanying the newlyweds on this southern progress would be many of their New York City belongings, among them carved Régence fauteuils, streamlined contemporary slipper chairs, and towering eighteenth-century Gothic Revival cabinets. Britt's challenge was to use these disparate ingredients in rooms to reflect the coastal city's salt-air ésprit and to be an ebullient backdrop for the young family.

Good cheer and graphic punchiness are the project's leitmotifs, offset by discreet and regionally suggestive dashes of seashells, tortoiseshell, and bamboo. The jumping-off point for the new decorating scheme easily could have been a pair of preppy madras shorts, given the kicky colors that Britt brought into play beneath the steep tray ceilings and amid pallid cypress paneling. A funky multicolor check combining blue, yellow, green, pink, and white upholsters the living room's trio of sofas, each laden with fat, pink throw cushions that match the clear rosy hues of a large abstract oil painting by Colombian artist Alvaro Herrán. Additional pink yardage softens the Régence cane-seated armchairs, which Britt coated with white paint as blithely as he blanched the Gothic Revival cabinets. Attenuated white floor lamps crowned with crisp card shades light the double-height room, a clutch of Britt-designed slipper chairs wears blue denim slipcovers, and diamond-pattern seagrass matting stretches across the terrazzo floor.

In the adjoining solarium, a framed antique
American quilt of polychrome stars and zigzag
stripes is the depth-charge focal point;
it is mounted behind a spacious U-shape
banquette that is dappled with yet more
large pink cushions.

Suffused with drama though largely bereft
of color is the fantastical dining room, a
contemporary evocation of the latticework
garden pavilions that ingenious French
treillageurs constructed in the seventeenth and
eighteenth centuries. (American tastemakers
Stanford White and Elsie de Wolfe revived the
technique to substantial acclaim in the early
1900s.) Britt romanced the otherwise modest
space with large sheets of mirrored glass that
are set within handmade white arches, pilasters,
and panels, their openwork details matched by
woven rattan armchairs modeled after an iconic
1930s chaise by Jean-Michel Frank and Adolphe
Chanaux. Reflected ad infinitum and grounded
by a pastel carpet, the airy installation
is the whimsical high point of a frolicsome,
family-friendly house by the sea.

KANSAS CITY · MISSOURI

1982

Powerful art requires a strong setting,
a decorating scheme that won't be overwhelmed by
the commanding character of the assembled paintings
and sculptures and also won't compete with them.
For a New Jersey–born artist who settled in Kansas City,
Missouri, after years of living and studying in Europe,
a certain symbiosis was his environmental preference.
The art—including examples of his own totemic metal pieces—
had to live in the client's 1920s apartment as
comfortably as he did. And the atmosphere had
to seem organic rather than imposed.

Britt produced an uncompromisingly masculine décor that channels the artist's own rangy, swaggering personality. It is also as stalwart as the art it complements, from an impassive Kono mask from Mali in the living room to a lethal-looking Mark Royer mobile that lazily oscillates in the study. Like a coat of Coromandel lacquer, oxblood-red paint enrobes the apartment's applied moldings and paneled doors, diminishing the period architectural details to mere texture. To effect a dramatic contrast to the walls, Britt scoured the wood floors to a pale finish. The result is almost industrial in its plainness and, appropriately enough, given the resident's career, reminiscent of those in loft buildings that have been turned into artist's studios.

The envelope may be uncomplicated, but
the décor within it possesses an animal
sensuality—intimate, coaxing, seductive.
Glove leather, boldly tufted, saddle-
stitched, and in a similar red as the walls,
upholsters the living room's long, low
banquettes as well as the homeowner's bed.
Tortoiseshell sheathes the Britt-designed
pedestal dining table, which the decorator
flanked with a quartet of graceful
Biedermeier side chairs that are cushioned
in the same leather. In classic Britt
tradition, table lamps are few. Rather,
track lighting directs shafts of illumination
throughout, setting a Mayan stone head,
a Korean chest, a sheet-steel sculpture
above the bed, and so much else all
dramatically aglow.

NEW YORK • NEW YORK

1979

Modern art grips and challenges: edgy in attitude, brilliantly colored, often outsize in its proportions and scale. When those characteristics are multiplied by several factors, conventional decorating elements, such as patterned fabrics and walls painted any color other than a shade of white, must be taken out of play.

For a New York City art connoisseur and his wife, Britt retrained his hallmark aesthetic exuberance to give center stage to the couple's provocative and cutting-edge contemporary masterworks, several of which have been included in major museum exhibitions. What else could he do? The impressive collection includes a 1964 Claes Oldenburg painted-wood sculpture in the form of a giant electrical outlet, a dizzying Jean Dubuffet acrylic-on-polyester-resin wall piece from the artist's Élément bleu series, Andy Warhol's 1961 *Five Coca-Cola Bottles*, a big gold Louise Nevelson assemblage, and a large Agnes Martin canvas whose polychrome surface—the earthy tones and geometric motifs bring Ghanaian kente cloth to mind—practically pulsates. Add pre-Columbian ceramics and Tulare and Apache baskets to that mix, and the challenge is obvious.

Britt thus treated the couple's apartment, located in a 1920s Park Avenue building designed by Japanese-American architect Yasuo Matsui, as a gallery for domestic bliss. The palette is dominated by white, though in softer shades than the art-world norm: on the featureless walls, the sleek vertical window blinds, the knubby carpets, and much of the primary seating. Against this blanched background, the art, each piece sensitively displayed for maximum effect and in its relationship to other works, stands out with riveting clarity.

The furnishings are treated as artful expressions, too. For the living room Britt selected pale-colored sofas and slipper chairs, all iconic models by Billy Baldwin, that are discreet in effect yet strongly sculptural in form. A handful of dark-wood antiques bring history and warmth to the apartment's ultramodern atmosphere, among them an array of lacy nineteenth- and twentieth-century Chinese tables (one of them hosts a stunning Mende *sowei* mask from Sierre Leone) and a neoclassical Louis XVI armchair (clad in rosewood-tone leather).

Britt may have been forced to work in unusually subdued fashion, but he managed to incorporate some subtly heroic gestures. Brass inlay turns the entrance hall's inky parquet into a dramatic field of diamonds. The same pattern, this time slightly larger in scale and executed with paint, crisscrosses the floors of a corridor and the master bedroom. And in the latter space, Britt lulls the owners to sleep with a prime example of his often-subversive chic: a plainly tailored bed upholstered entirely in brown leather, right down to the coverlet.

WELLESLEY · MASSACHUSETTS

1992

Suburbia, as a word and as a location, rarely inspires.
But some otherwise nondescript homes constructed near major metropolitan centers often
conceal extraordinary interiors that blend familial coziness, dashing style, and exceptional art.
One such residence, not far from Boston, has twice received the Britt treatment.

Connoisseurs of colorful, cutting-edge art, the clients first reached out to the designer in the 1970s, asking him to conjure up a décor that would enhance their fast-growing collection of gutsy, graphic modern and contemporary art by masters such as Jules Olitski, Jack Youngerman, Donald Judd, Roy Lichtenstein, and Jasper Johns. Twenty years after that first art-emphasizing renovation—when Britt painted walls and ceilings white, installed white carpeting, added tailored but temptingly plump white upholstery, and hung white plantation shutters at some windows—the designer came back to undertake a gentle update.

The second time around Britt brought
greater depth and a subtle sheen to the
alabaster décor, which the couple had
enjoyed and preferred to leave relatively
unchanged. Shining paint and lacquer
visually heighten the rooms' challenged
ceilings and expand the square footage
while enhancing the glow cast by the
recessed ceiling fixtures. Textured white
and off-white fabrics—velvety checks,
crisp chevron weaves, orderly quilted
grids—outfit Britt's custom-made sofas,
banquettes, and ottomans. Off-white
brickwork-pattern carpets floor the
living and dining rooms. Britt exotica,
from Asian low tables in the living room
to a Parsons-style sofa table sheathed
in mottled horn, balances the couple's
handful of eighteenth-century American,
English, and Welsh antiques.

Contemporary in attitude yet grounded in history, Britt's subtly improved décor acknowledges the New England setting while downshifting the designer's fast-forward sensibility to a domestic speed.

HISTORICAL

PAST MEETS PRESENT • ANTIQUES WITH AN EDGE
ROMANCE AND RIGOR

NEW YORK • NEW YORK

1990

New York City town houses have notoriously short
single-owner lifespans. Personal fortunes ebb, fashionable
neighborhoods lose their exclusivity, and an elegant
residence that was proudly constructed as a monument
to one family's success becomes a multi-tenant warren,
carved up into rentable sections.

Located on the parlor floor of a Beaux-Arts mansion
constructed in 1903 by architects James R. Turner and
William G. Killian, the one-bedroom apartment of a
young fashion manufacturing executive is one of these
awkward slices. Long and narrow, the layout recalls
nothing more than an upmarket railroad flat. Britt,
working with his associate Malcolm McKinstrie II, gave
the apartment's three rooms—an entrance hall flanked
by a master bedroom and a multipurpose living room—
the nobility it signally lacked, conjuring up a haute
Parisian fantasy that is far more elaborate than Turner
and Killian ever imagined, but which seems
an appropriate response to the building's palatial
French-informed facade.

A faux-stone treatment finishes the plaster walls, giving them the appearance of sugary blocks of the Lutetian limestone that gives the French capital its golden glow. Antique Régence double doors—highly carved with crowns, shields, and fluttering ribbons and bleached to a pale-honey pallor—bring to mind the exquisite Paris mansions that were built during the same period as the Manhattan town house and in similar emulation of the past, such as the Musée Nissim de Camondo.

The furnishings, many of them acquired in Europe, heighten the Continental effect. And though they add a certain period flavor, they do not re-create any particular moment in aesthetic time, partly because of Britt's modern attitude. From the living room's low, floor-hugging contemporary sofa—which seems informed by both Coco Chanel's famous version and Ottoman divans—to the neoclassical side chairs in the entrance hall, almost everything is cushioned in camel-color velvet or leather, rather than jewel-tone damasks and brocades. Only a pair of giltwood crossed-sword stools topped with a leopard-spot velvet, a version of the famous 1805 design that architect Bernard Poyet created for the freshly crowned Emperor Napoléon, is the exception to that rule.

Within this warm amber-tone envelope, at once neutral and sybaritic, Britt assembled his broad-shouldered European finds: First Empire candelabra incorporating winged figures of Nike, the Greek goddess of victory; a bust of Napoléon; an immense Georgian knife urn that tops a mahogany center table often used for dining; and black-and-white engravings on classical themes, from Roman statuary to incense burners to obelisks. Serious, aristocratic, and serene, the effect is that of a gentleman connoisseur's lair.

NEW YORK · NEW YORK

1993

A lifelong student of design history, Britt always
has been enraptured by the theatrical work of French
architects and designers Charles Percier and Pierre Fontaine,
who gave Napoléon Bonaparte's reign its glittering martial
chic. Britt is particularly intrigued by the opulent and
soft architecture of the influential tented rooms that Percier
and Fontaine created for Napoléon and Joséphine at Château
de Malmaison. Emulating the emperor's campaign tents,
as well as those that he used on hunting trips,
Britt has adopted fabric-draped spaces as an integral
part of his own decorative vocabulary.

One of Britt's smallest such evocations is the Manhattan apartment of one of his assistants, who, perhaps not coincidentally, happens to be half French. The designer tented the second-floor home, a solution that offers a sense of romantic itinerancy— one can imagine the "tent" being taken down, rolled up, and pitched elsewhere. The voluminous layering also has the practical effect of muffling the sound of traffic on the busy street.

Hundreds of yards of pale peach cotton are gathered across ceilings and walls, variously parted to reveal either the windows or space-enhancing panels of mirrored glass. Notched valances edged with black-and-white passementerie trace the cornice line, with the same trim finishing the cushions of the bed and banquettes. Statues and busts emphasize the intimate imperial air, while Chinese rosewood tables and stools, inlaid with sparkling mother-of-pearl, seem to melt into the bare, ebony-stained floor.

NEW YORK • NEW YORK

1992

One of Britt's clients proved as strong a character
as the designer himself: powerful, tenacious,
calm in demeanor but imperial in impact. A real estate
developer and philanthropist of the first rank, he and his
wife settled on the topmost floor of a residential tower
with a reputation for its concentration of major moguls.

Stately and urbane, the apartment is designed for entertaining. It serves as a backdrop to high-powered gatherings of business partners and fellow philanthropists, to posh cocktail parties, and to grand dinners. And the décor, with furnishings that bring to mind Bourbons and Bonapartes, makes unmistakably clear that the couple are Manhattan monarchs.

Much of the apartment is given over to a majestically scaled living-dining area, some sixty feet long, which is monochromatic yet full of bold contrasts. Snow-white walls and ceilings offset silken fabrics of red and pink, in shades ranging from azalea to shocking. White custom-made sofas, grandly scaled and dripping with matching fringe, anchor multiple seating areas that are outfitted with regal early nineteenth-century European antiques, such as a pair of Charles X armchairs and a low table of the same period. Art is reduced to the minimum, the walls hosting little more than rhythmic rows of antique etchings that depict ancient Greek and Roman busts.

Other echoes of the glorious past include neoclassical figures that hold aloft etched lanterns in the living area or are incorporated into a multitude of Empire gilt-bronze table lamps; a period bust of Napoléon, placed at the center of a nineteenth-century Swedish writing table, surveys the all-white master bedroom.

NEW YORK • NEW YORK

1997

Bachelor pads are typically relinquished
when marriage enters the picture. But when the scion of
a family-owned coat manufacturer wed a fashion executive,
the couple chose to share the groom's Britt-decorated town
house apartment (see pages 124–31). That space had an
intimate and opulent Parisian atmosphere, one that was
expanded—and in one area, invitingly ignored—after the
young couple acquired the first and ground floors of the
early twentieth-century building.

With architectural designer Peter Napolitano, Britt recalibrated and regularized the floor plan, which had been ham-fistedly divided into multiple apartments over time. The bachelor bedroom became the dining room, with Empire-style chairs that Britt reproduced from a period original.

The bed, armchairs, and other furnishings
from the former bedroom now live downstairs
in a bedroom-cum-library that is wrapped
with scarlet velvet, some of it stamped,
some of it plain. A jewel box for sleeping and
reading, it features a graceful mahogany spiral
staircase that Napolitano designed—after the
originals at Château de Groussay, twentieth-
century tastemaker Carlos de Beistegui's
influential country house near Paris—
to navigate the apartment's three levels.

Britt's lifetime love of Empire-style tented rooms is expressed in the cream-curtained study, which echoes a fabric-draped apartment that the designer had created around the same time for one of his assistants. Here, however, Britt's appreciation for unique period oddities gives the study an entirely distinctive feeling. Bizarre antique Austrian chairs topped with gilded eagles—seemingly straddling the stylistic line between Empire and Biedermeier—are upholstered in lemon-yellow fabric, and immense electrified torchères weight the neoclassical writing table, their improbable enormity drawing the eye up to a shell-shape pendant light, which casts a soft glow across the tray ceiling.

Meager architecture—tentative moldings, spindly columns, milquetoast baseboards—is one of Britt's favorite challenges, allowing him the opportunity to scrape bare and then ennoble. A residence located in the leafy Buckhead neighborhood of Atlanta was one such opportunity: a freshly built redbrick blend of styles, partly Georgian Revival, partly French manoir, with interior detailing that lacked any discernable oomph.

The clients had been seduced by European neoclassicism of the early nineteenth century, from First Empire flash to the brawny equivalent espoused across the English Channel by Thomas Hope, and were already purchasing furniture of that period—such as a Biedermeier secretary and English Regency center table—when they hired Britt to devise an appropriately muscular background. Existing columns were beefed up, moldings were broadened, and arches were punctuated with keystones. Walls were painted to resemble large blocks of limestone and marble, and the floors of the living room and the adjoining solarium were bleached and then stained with giant diamonds.

Britt, always a flouter of rules, insouciantly glamorized the English Regency double-pedestal dining table by gilding its carved feet and lesser details—all the better for it to coordinate with the Empire chairs and Charles X candelabra. There is wit, too: in the library, a pair of tortoiseshell guéridons seems to grow out of the similarly spotted leopard-print carpet.

Britt encouraged the clients in their collecting, helping them to expand their neoclassical fascinations and to see how works from later periods could perfectly complement their nineteenth-century treasures. Thus, the breakfast room's gilded Empire side chairs, upholstered in black-and-white awning stripe, surround an Art Deco walnut table, and the living room is dappled with mod tortoiseshell cocktail tables, which were designed by Britt.

The bedroom follows stylistic suit,
though in intimate fashion, its echoes
of the past given modern freshness
with a crisp palette of white and gold.

NEW YORK • NEW YORK

1992

Two characteristics readily associated with
Britt's decors are monumentality and classicism.
Both are rooted in his fascination with the grandeur
of the ancient world, from the Acropolis in Athens to
the Forum in Rome. In fact, as he has matured as
a designer, he often notes how much more muscular
and imperial his taste has become. Columns are erected,
immense cornices ring ceilings, and stone-look
finishes are a regular occurrence.

Consider the apartment that Britt created for
his longtime contractor. The flat, located in a
late nineteenth-century tenement building in
Manhattan's Lenox Hill neighborhood, is dark,
with two sets of windows facing a backyard.
Working with the resident contractor, who
handled all the construction and paintwork,
Britt remodeled the space and installed a
theatrical décor that recalls a neo-Romantic set
for a Sophocles play or, perhaps, a small temple
in Asia Minor converted for domestic use.

Faux-marble trickery coats every wall
and bookcase, as well as lightweight wood
elements—cubes, slabs, and the like—
that can be ingeniously assembled into
tables for a variety of purposes. The
unprepossessing windows, now dressed in
filmy white swags, have been built out to
create tall niches: in the living area niche,
Britt has placed one of several stupendous
pedestals topped with magnificent spheres,
to emphasize the height of the ceilings; and
in the bedroom niche, Britt has placed a
classical bust. Mirrors embedded in various
walls are a paramount decorative element,
several of them facing another in order
to expand the interiors' dimensions,
in effect generating endless enfilades.

Britt also designed massive banquettes that he covered with pale Thai silk. Those upholstered pieces, though eminently comfortable, look like hefty blocks of marble, relieved by Empire-style and Louis XV–inspired chairs and attenuated Spanish Renaissance candlesticks.

2001

When architectural details don't exist or fail to inspire, Britt supplies them,
often installing grand cornices and noble columns. For a pied-à-terre at the former
Westbury Hotel facing Manhattan's Central Park, Britt implied them through
painted finishes that are of a piece with the décor they surround.

The apartment, owned by a Tokyo-based mother and son,
has no architecture worth mentioning—and even less after the building,
constructed in 1927, was converted into condominiums in 1999.
Decorative artist Dmitry Dudnik did Britt's trompe-l'oeil bidding,
brushing the walls with simple stiles and rails that organize and
ennoble the rooms while providing symmetrical fields for Britt-designed
mirrors and architectural engravings.

The dragged paintwork—reminiscent of that in tastemaker Nancy Lancaster's charming bedroom in London and her business partner John Fowler's entrance hall at his Hampshire country place—gives the apartment a quiet, landed-gentry air that befits the elegant furnishings. Britt's clients already owned a beautiful Regency double-pedestal dining table, and its sober elegance, darkly finished yet sparklingly gilded, is reflected throughout the traditional décor, where chalky tones of gray, blue, and taupe predominate and a largely Anglophile attitude prevails. Regency-style bookcases filled with worn leather-bound books flank the doorway between the living and dining rooms.

Neoclassical-style consoles that recall the kind of furniture English aristocrats brought back from the Grand Tour are positioned in the entrance hall and in an adjacent corridor, each of them flanked with lean side chairs of Directoire mien. A few Asian pieces, among them a magnificent armoire in the master bedroom and a sinewy Chinese lacquer sideboard in the dining room, add a cosmopolitan touch.

CLASSIC

TIMELESS ALLURE • SWAGGER SILHOUETTES
AESTHETIC AUTHORITY

MISSION HILLS · KANSAS

1999

In the 1990s, husband-and-wife civic leaders in Kansas City decided to sell their large
suburban family house (see pages 218–25)—which had been redecorated by Britt in the early 1980s—
in favor of an empty-nest residence that was far more manageable in size and scale.
What the clients settled on was charming, relatively modest, and dated from the 1970s.
Shaped like an *H* and spread across one level, its sole architectural delight was an entrance
courtyard enclosed by two projecting wings and a low wall.

With the change in address came striking changes in palette and structure. Faced with banal interiors, Britt raised numerous rooms to the rafters, establishing great vaulted spaces whose vertical theatricality is belied by the building's milquetoast countenance. (His partners in this spatial transformation were architectural designer Peter Napolitano, a longtime Britt associate, and regional architects Nearing, Staats, Prelogar & Jones.) Cornices were beefed up, moldings were applied to create dramatic panels that gave a châteauesque aspect to walls and ceilings, mantels were refinished and ennobled with gilded ornamentation, and marble floors were laid.

Many of the furnishings moved with the clients to the smaller house, though not without alterations. Britt reupholstered everything he could, from sofas to slipper chairs, resulting in an energetic new décor that still had familiar underpinnings. Flower-tone salmons, pinks, and greens give way to crisp black and white in stripes, diamonds, checks, and toiles de Jouy. Even the dining chairs, formerly dark wood, have been repainted chalk white. Only the star-pattern Indian dhurries in the living and dining rooms made the journey across town unchanged.

Both the living and dining rooms are
magnified by two-story arched mirrors
placed on opposite walls. A similarly
shaped new window dominates the peach-
and-coral master bedroom, where it is
flanked by towering bookcases shaped like
obelisks. The bedroom's paneled ceiling
is a stripped-down version of one that
George Oakes and John Fowler created—
in trompe l'oeil rather than moldings—
for Haseley Court, Nancy Lancaster's
Oxfordshire country house.

SAN FRANCISCO • CALIFORNIA

2009

The San Francisco living room of two young movers-and-shakers fulfills the dashing couple's desire for a grand and glamorous space.

Britt brought in claret-red velvet stamped with a damask pattern to cover the walls and two vast button-tufted sofas. Black and white are the living room's other chromatic tones, the darkness of the black intensifying the ruddy surrounds while the clarity of the white lends lightness. Black is the solo tone for the obsidian-dark wood floor, the poured-resin center table, and the Britt-designed armchairs, while black and white meet in the club chairs' diaper-pattern upholstery, a quartet of Indian inlaid-bone tables, and slender consoles that host florid porcelain candelabras. All around, selections from the husband's photography collection are displayed, including Japanese artist Hiroshi Sugimoto's mesmerizing portrait of a waxwork replica of Queen Elizabeth II.

PALM BEACH · FLORIDA

1988

By their very nature, second homes are escapist affairs, places to get away and live life differently for a while. A real estate developer and his wife, for example, spent most of the year in a Normandy-inspired house in Mission Hills, a stately suburb of Kansas City. When temperatures dropped, the couple shifted their focus to Palm Beach, Florida, where Britt decorated their three-bedroom apartment at Dunster House, an eccentrically stylish black-and-white building facing the Atlantic Ocean.

The designer's splashy neoclassical-style décor—one might describe it as Palazzo Mod—is as snow white as the exterior of Dunster House, with similar dark highlights and touches of brass and gold. In the thirty-foot-long L-shape living room, overstuffed white sofas clad in a voluptuous basket-weave chenille stand on a wood floor that has been painted to mimic white marble inset with black diamonds and circles. Britt used the geometric pattern throughout the apartment and copied it from the entrance hall at Vizcaya, the great Miami mansion that architect F. Burrall Hoffman Jr. planned in the early 1900s for industrialist James Deering.

Exuberant black-and-gold chairs modeled after an original by Thomas Hope, the English Regency architect and designer, are used throughout the main entertaining spaces, including the mirror-walled dining area, a long and narrow space (11.5 feet long by 9.5 feet wide) where Britt installed two modern faux-granite pedestal tables that he designed. Instead of curtains, sliding panels with vertical slats temper the bright subtropical light and stripe the interior with intriguing shadows. When the panels are parted, blue sky and crashing waves are reflected in mirrors large and small.

The master bedroom, on the other hand, is almost entirely white. Ebony accents are drastically reduced, and the hard chic of the living room and dining area has been transformed into pillowy softness. An extravagantly curtained bed anchors the space, and a diamond-quilted fabric covers the headboard and armchairs. Though the interior is unmistakably contemporary, atmospheric antiques serve as operatic exclamation points, most prominently a queenly wood bust that surveys the room from a baroque wall bracket.

NEW YORK • NEW YORK

1997

In a daring departure from the deluxe show-house norm, Britt's dining room for the 1997 Kips Bay Decorator Show House feels purposefully unfinished. Walls and ceiling are meticulously grained to resemble raw plywood. The floor is paved with creamy wall-to-wall sisal, the fine weave seemingly a continuation of the decorative graining while the scratchy, utilitarian texture adds to the relaxed air: When, one wonders, will the carpet arrive?

As for the furnishings, they make strange bedfellows at first glance, as if each was pulled out of the designer's warehouse and are awaiting approval. But the mingled periods and overscale silhouettes—nearly every item is hefty, as well as sculptural—purposefully contribute to the impromptu atmosphere. The tall Queen Anne dining chairs, upholstered in a sulfurous shade of yellow leather, have shapely, deeply canted backs that invite lazy, end-of-dinner postures. A towering wall clock in vivid coral faces a grandiose octagonal sunburst mirror on the opposite side of the room, while curious chinoiserie panels with pagoda silhouettes hang above Chinese Chippendale consoles. Matching objects— Chinese vessels, white-capped candlestick lamps, bull's-eye mirrors, and double gourd vases—add rhythm and, in some cases, provide the illusion of length, like virtual vanishing points.

MISSION HILLS • KANSAS

2003

For Britt, color is the key to a house: to its presentation,
to its life, to its personality. He often starts with one hue
and handles it as a composer would a musical theme—
amplifying it in one room and toning it down in another,
exploring the panoply of possibilities from pianissimo
to fortissimo. What results is a house that projects an
air of serenity and inevitability, as one room flows into
another, each possessing its singular personality and
purpose while remaining fully related.

When Britt was asked to decorate a brand new
Georgian-style residence in the American Midwest,
the designer settled on blue and white, a favorite
combination of the young clients. But instead
of delivering a fresh-faced décor that is long on
cheerfulness and short on depth, Britt (working with
longtime associates Valentino Samsonadze, Cathleen
Quinlan Hodgson, and Peter Napolitano) developed a
series of inviting rooms that adhere to the color scheme
while offering a multitude of moods.

The living room, for example, goes to the dark end of the chromatic spectrum, featuring navy-blue-and-white fabrics woven with outsize checks and stripes and a jazzy color-coordinated Indian dhurrie that adds a warming note of saffron.

Saffron, again, is picked up in the dining room, where shiny sunshine walls meet additional blue-and-white textiles, including complementary stripes that curtain the windows and cushion the eighteenth-century English chairs. Another dhurrie, this time largely blue relieved by a thin tracery of white, covers the floor.

Rounding out Britt's varied cerulean schemes are carefully calibrated accessories. Table lamps are fashioned from vessels made of blue-and-white Chinese porcelain or candlesticks of white milk glass. Chinese cachepots and vases, also blue-and-white ceramic, sit on baroque pedestals and a neoclassical-style serving table. Blue ceramic dishes occupy Asian occasional tables, and at the center of the library's cocktail table sits a grace note, one that is small in size but riveting in tone: a single nineteenth-century opaline box so brilliantly and intensely blue—the shade is known as *bleu celeste*—that it appears to be lit from the inside.

Pale sky blue is painted onto the study's walls and vaulted ceiling; its vaporousness is strengthened by the presence of a striped dhurrie that is woven in two deeper shades of blue alternating with white. More blues decorate the master bedroom, ranging from denim to near-periwinkle, and the motifs include miniscule diamonds for the sofa cushions and an awning-style stripe applied to the shapely headboard.

MISSION HILLS·KANSAS

1985

The house built in 1923 for oil refining magnate
Louis L. Marcell embodies Midwestern prosperity:
sturdy redbrick walls topped with a mottled clay-tile roof—
Jazz Age Tuscan is the best description possible—paneled
rooms, an arched loggia, and a stone terrace where stairs
descend to formal hedged gardens. The interiors hued
largely to traditional antiques and classic flowered fabrics
for decades, but later owners called on Britt to install
a fresher décor, livelier and less conventional than the one
they had lived with for so long.

Daylily shades of coral, orange, and pink—all silk fabrics,
some striped, others solid—bring a blush to the living
room, offset by the sofas' upholstery, a thyme-green velvet
that has been luxuriously gauffraged, or stamped, with
opulent and overlarge flowers and medallions. The latter
touch is just one of the artful, energizing exaggerations that
Britt deployed in his aesthetic rejuvenation.

Hearty valances top many of the windows;
the living room's are trimmed with
bittersweet-orange and shell-pink ribbons
that terminate in winsome rosettes. For the
living room and dining room floor, Britt,
a passionate admirer of Indian culture,
commissioned expansive dhurries woven
with stars and crosses. The gutsy geometric
pattern is the designer's woven-wool
evocation of an eighteenth-century marble
floor at Suraj Bhawan, a mansion that is
part of the Bharatpur maharajahs' Deeg
Palace complex in Rajasthan. Shimmer and
shine come into play in the living room, too,
through an assortment of small, dark, and
lacy occasional tables inlaid with mother-
of-pearl, a favorite Britt touch.

The solarium is painted a deep glossy green, a shade that echoes the trees outside and gives the room the feeling of a virtual forest. Earthy tones of coral, as well as a graphic fabric with a Silk Road attitude, link this more masculine space to the house's primary palette, and a handful of Asian accents—scroll paintings, a chess set, a coffee table—add a well-traveled air.

Asian treasures are, in fact, a subtle leitmotif throughout the house. Antique Chinese dolls can be found displayed on a stair landing, while a ceramic Buddha centers an old Venetian table in the living room, not far from a sofa accented by a decorative cushion embroidered in 1920s chinoiserie style. As for the dining room, its pink-and-orange walls are a cheerful background for a series of framed Chinese scroll paintings.

LADUE · MISSOURI

2010

Houses with a Georgian mien typically command
similarly classic interiors: a little bit formal and
enormously safe. Britt's approach has always been
to shake up the tried-and-true, to give traditionalism
a kick in the pants, and to bring contemporary
effervescence to a style of architecture that, in its day,
was as up-to-date as any fashion-conscious
homeowner could have wanted.

Relevance, not reverence, was in the forefront of
Britt's mind when a growing young family living not far
from St. Louis, Missouri, commissioned the designer to
redecorate their eighteenth-century-inflected house—
which, to Britt's surprise, had started out as a relatively
humble farmhouse more than a hundred years ago.
Gunn & Smith, a St. Louis architecture firm, had twice
made alterations to the original building, transforming
it into a white-painted brick mansion with French doors
topped with fanlights and an entrance porch trimmed
with a Chinese Chippendale–inspired railing.
With that stylistic invention firmly in mind, Britt
had no interest in delivering a rote exploration
of landed-gentry elegance.

The living room's bright blend of lemon-yellow walls, Régence armchairs upholstered in lipstick-red velvet, and a smoke-blue sofa and loveseats—complemented by Louise Nevelson prints and a room-size Indian dhurrie in similar color combinations—makes a jazzy setting for cocktails. The nearby dining room is its absolute opposite, with walls painted a green so dark that it reads as black, like certain Chinese jades infused with iron ore. It is a murky shade that instantly affects a transformational hush as one enters the space, where Britt has established a bracing tension by pitting the peaceful old against the dynamic new. At the center, an obsidian-dark dining table ringed by aristocratic white-and-gold Directoire-style chairs—so far, so chic—is overlooked by a towering, tempestuous silkscreen that is one of avant-garde Chinese artist Qin Feng's dynamic takes on ancient calligraphy.

"What this house wanted was style, energy, and color," Britt once said— and though he intended to bring European antiques into the decorative mix, he also put modern American and Asian art on his shopping list. Ditto capacious rolled-arm sofas and broad-bottomed armchairs (for comfort), carpets both vigorously patterned and gloriously carved (to provide animation and texture), and powerhouse paint colors that, when daringly juxtaposed, would emphasize the rooms' uses as well as their intended energy.

Equally energizing, though in far more subtle tones, is the pool pavilion. There, beneath a beamed and vaulted ceiling, Britt conjures up a tropical vibe—but using only shades of gold, taupe, and coconut brown, as if Coco Chanel had decided to put her smoky stamp on a Caribbean isle. Printed in metallic gold on crisp white, the famous banana-leaf-print cotton that Dorothy McNab designed decades ago for her decorator sister Rose Cumming causes the upholstered furnishings' strict silhouettes to melt away into a virtual jungle. That feeling is amplified by the leafy brass chandelier and matching mirror, voluptuous shell-shape plaster sconces, and statuettes in the form of exotic fish that seem to lazily swim atop the kitchen's cabinets.

233

AT HOME

NEW YORK • NEW YORK

1985

For more than forty years, Britt has called one
of New York City's most romantic interiors home: a
triplex apartment carved out of an Upper East Side
mansion that dates to 1901. The exceptionally aristocratic
interiors remained almost entirely intact when the house
was converted into multiple dwellings, and Britt got the
best of the lot—opulent, high-ceilinged spaces paved with
marble and parquet and wrapped
with elaborate paneling.

How he decorated this envelope of architectural
pastry work both honors its history and updates its
spirit. The oval library, located on the main level, fast-
forwards history into contemporary times. Britt blithely
bleached the Louis XV–style boiseries to faintest honey
and refinished the parquet floor with a two-tone zigzag
pattern. Hearty and sculptural upholstered sofas and
chairs dressed in purest white Thai cotton fill the room,
while towering custom-made bookcases with pagoda tops
contain books that are bound in parchment-color jackets
to blend into the palette, as do an assortment of sugary,
classical marble busts.

The adjoining dining room is just as colorless, with faux-marble walls surrounding a table that Britt designed and had veneered with tortoiseshell. In this tall, long, narrow space, though, the decorator has conjured up a monumental air, as if he'd sliced off a corner of Versailles and repurposed it. Sheets of mirror expand the space while reflecting two heroic marble atlantes—bracket-like representations of Atlas, the Greek divinity—that flank yet another mirror, this one an enormous giltwood Chinese Chippendale fantasia that was formerly owned by the decorator Rose Cumming, one of the young Britt's mentors and inspirations.

The main floor's cool pallor gives way to nightclub drama in the former music room on the floor above. Here, Britt coated the paneling, which is even more elaborate than the living room's, with a shade of aubergine so deep that it's nearly black. Mirrored panels, doors, and fanlights—most of the silvery glass was added by Britt—transforms the largely candlelit space into an idiosyncratic iteration of Versailles's Hall of Mirrors, though it is louche and seductive rather than sunny and bright. Lightweight Regency armchairs of black and gold mingle with brawny upholstered pieces that, depending on the designer's mood, are slipcovered in either white cotton or dark blue satin.

By comparison, the apartment's third
level, which contains little more than
Britt's no-color bedroom, is absolutely
monastic, a repudiation of the grandeur
downstairs—though, Britt being Britt,
his sleeping chamber is the acme of
luxury. A silk-curtained bed, like a room
within a room, centers the space, while
mirrored glass paves the walls, creating
an infinity of reflections that belie the
cramped square footage.

WATER MILL • NEW YORK

1998

Given Britt's fascination with grand historical
architecture, it was only a matter of time before he put
that passion into practice in a building project for himself.
Wanting to create a larger house that would be the
centerpiece of his Long Island acreage, he reinterpreted
Warsaw's Biały Domek, or Little White House, an
exquisitely proportioned 1778 neoclassical villa, perfectly
square and only five bays wide, that architect Domenico
Merlini had modeled on Versailles's Petit Trianon.

Achieved with architects Peter Cook and Doug Moyer,
Britt's replica of the Polish masterwork is made of wood
rather than stucco, with a rusticated facade topped with
sprightly urns. The interiors, created with the input of
associates Peter Napolitano, Valentino Samsonadze, and
Ryszard Chmielewski, are grounded in the past, too,
but globetrot between the most unlikely locales, from
Gustavian Sweden to ancient Burma.

The double-length central living area—a vast space that is part library, part drawing room—owes a debt to Château de Groussay, tastemaker Carlos de Beistegui's house near Paris. The spiral staircases that architect Emilio Terry created for Beistegui's library inspired Britt's own, though the latter were executed in painted metal—originally in black, and later in white—rather than polished mahogany. They are set into a lighthearted room where pollen-yellow walls meet orange leather upholstery, engravings with sky-blue mats, and floor lamps with shiny red shades and golden bases in the form of bamboo.

The spectacular dining room seems
to meld Jacobean England and Burmese
holy sites; indeed, the immense mirrored
panel that dominates the space
came from a Southeast Asian temple.

Then there is the breakfast room (overleaf), arguably one of the most beautiful interiors that Britt ever created: its walls are painted with extravagant blue-and-white chinoiserie landscapes that channel the appropriately named Porcelain Kitchen at Tureholms Slott, a mid-eighteenth-century Swedish country house.

The Nordic spirit extends into the sitting room, where blue-and-white-striped banquettes line two-tone blue walls that are hung with violet-matted seascapes. Whitewashed Chinese tables blend into the Gustavian-inspired scheme, as do low Indian tables in a similar tone.

Britt's neoclassical invention—now owned
by clients who have preserved the interiors
with near-religious zeal—is a stage set
of sorts, a folly, composed of a theatrical
chronology of past styles that have been
insouciantly combined and updated
for the present day. What keeps these
disparate environments from confusion and
dissonance is that each has been developed
as a powerful aesthetic statement, strongly
colored, grandly patterned, and with a
similar sense of scale to the space that
comes before and the space that follows.

WATER MILL • NEW YORK

1991

The Long Island barn that Britt and his then wife, Julie, fell in love with in the 1960s belonged to a friend and could only be used in warm months. But what it lacked—insulation and weathertight windows—it made up for in romance. Sliding screen doors opened the barn to passing breezes, and Mexican masons had built a sculptural mantel in the main room, where lacy white-painted Burmese and Indian furniture stood on cool slate paving. Two little bedrooms made the place a tidy weekend and summer destination.

The Britts eventually planned a Water Mill getaway in emulation of the barn they admired, even constructing it around the salvaged superstructure of an eighteenth-century barn, but made it a year-round destination. Though the house seems much the same as that long-ago friend's place—with white walls, slate floor painted glossy black, and glass windows and sliding doors in the place of the screens—its sophistication significantly departs from its relatively rustic inspiration.

In Britt's living area, white quilted-vinyl sofas
are arranged in front of a cunning fireplace
that is topped by a window framing trees
and sky. (That unusual opening, inspired by
a French Empire example rooted in Britt's
memory, is achieved by diverting the flue.)
The designer's passion for multiples creates
peaceful rhythms, from the parade of matching
seashells, candlesticks, and zinnia-packed
vases marching across the mantel to the
symmetrically arranged floor lamps, the latter
so attenuated as to practically disappear.
Potted plants, including a fiddle leaf fig and
a couple of rubber trees, arch overhead,
the jungle-like profusion contrasting with
the bucolic farm fields nearby.

Though the cedar-shingled structure
is architecturally simple, inside and out,
Britt elevates it with daredevil gestures.
The front door is crowned by a theatrically
overscale broken pediment. An attic guest
bedroom hosts a scarlet canopy bed that
soars so high it seems like something
out of a fantastic Renaissance painting.
Britt's own room, on the ground floor,
is a Mughal daydream, the walls layered
with a metallic wallpaper whose fretwork
pattern is taken from Indian jali screens,
and the bed curtained with raucously
polychrome Indian tapestries appliquéd
with birds, flowers, and animals.

As is often the case, Britt's attention
to bedrooms results in domestic drama.
The designer's own suite is an orientalist
wonderland, where a canopy bed curtained
with flamboyant polychrome embroideries
is surrounded by silver-pattern ceiling and
walls, the latter arranged with colorful prints
depicting Indian and Persian nobles. Shades of
black and white come together in a guest room
(overleaf), the positive-negative color scheme
allowing a dramatic Japanese scroll painting,
a dynamic Wiener Werkstätte–reminiscent
mirror, and a wallpaper densely but delicately
patterned with flowering vines to coalesce
into a refreshing whole. Upstairs is the pièce
de résistance, slumber-wise (pages 278–79):
a raftered attic bedroom equipped with a
towering, elongated canopy bed that has
been lacquered a brilliant tomato red.

The coziest spot in the house is the
sitting room, a small but high space that,
with typical panache, Britt has painted
glossy black and has densely packed with
ranks of antique architectural renderings
of columns, chimneypieces, door
surrounds, and arches. A pair of carved-
wood Ionic capitals serves as cocktail
tables, and a delirious architectural
model—purchased when the designer
was a youth—rounds out the theme.

WATER MILL · NEW YORK

1997

Reached through a magnificent allée of cherry trees,
Britt's Long Island guesthouse—developed with his
associate Valentino Samsonadze and society architect
Peter Cook—appears quite simple. The form is plain
and entirely uncomplicated, shaped rather like a barbell:
an octagonal bedroom is linked by a long central hall
to an octagonal living room, which can serve
as another sleeping space.

Cedar shingles clad the one-story building's exterior,
making it seem as settled into the landscape as any
farmhouse. A simple white balustrade, somewhat like
a traditional widow's walk, lightens the roofline.
And every window is a French door, allowing the
structure to be entered from any direction while
giving it a pavilion-like sensibility.

Step through any of those double doors, though, and New England sobriety fades away, replaced by Orientalist exuberance set beneath steeply raked ceilings that echo the domes in imperial Ottoman architecture. Britt's memories of a long-ago visit to Malta's Casa Rocca Piccola, the noble Piro family's sixteenth-century mansion, inform the décor's candied-almond palette, where chalky shades of wine red, pale coral, bittersweet orange, and shell pink are cooled by touches of turquoise and lilac.

Britt's love of shimmer is seen throughout every room in the guesthouse. Indian chairs sheathed in embossed white metal stand alongside subcontinental chests inlaid with mother-of-pearl, and every coral wall hosts colorful Indian prints that are surrounded by silver checkerboard mats and simple silver-leaf frames. Even the nineteenth-century Chinese tables, carved with a palm tree motif, have been given a metallic finish.

WATER MILL • NEW YORK

1991

Outside, on the wide green lawn, stands the property's
most exotic fillip: a Moroccan tent, a highflying,
Orientalist folly set in the middle of what was once one
of the area's ubiquitous potato fields. Inside the tent—
erected seasonally and recalling the eighteenth-century
Turkish-style metal tents at Drottningholm Palace and
Château de Groussay—all is red, green, and gold, glitter
and glamour, the aureate glow of massed candles and
lanterns illuminating friends and family who eat, drink,
and lounge late into summer evenings.

BECOMING TOM BRITT

At the beginning, there was a tree. Actually, it wasn't at the beginning, but given Tom Britt's long career—more than fifty years—as one of America's most iconoclastic interior designers, it's a good place to start. And the tree wasn't literally a tree. It was his evocation of a tree, an artful child's attempt to make the ugly beautiful.

Spotting the furnace in his parents' Kansas City, Missouri, basement one day, Britt decided to scrub down the industrial hunk of sooty metal, get out his brushes and paints, and begin laying on color. What he composed still is talked about today as a defining moment by family and friends: an apple tree in full roseate bloom, the furnace consumed and obscured beneath green leaves, pink flowers, and red fruit. Like so much of Britt's work as a design impresario, the tree was a fantasy, an escape, an alternate reality that had nothing to do with the comfortable house that he shared with his parents and younger brother, their prosperous neighborhood, or even Kansas City. Instead the tree spoke of a world far away from that basement, a world that Britt would become part of, learn from, and then shake up with his singular, sensational vision.

For decades, Britt has made the mundane magical and essayed every style imaginable: modern rooms with museum-quality contemporary art,

CLOCKWISE, FROM UPPER LEFT: A DECORATING-THEMED DRAWING BY TOM BRITT, AGE SIXTEEN.
OUTSIDE HIS CHILDHOOD HOME IN KANSAS CITY, MISSOURI, 1942. AN INTERIOR STUDY EXECUTED AT PARSONS
SCHOOL OF DESIGN, CIRCA 1957. BRITT WITH HIS WIFE, JULIE, AT THE GREAT PYRAMID OF GIZA, EGYPT, 1970.
THE SEAFARING BRITTS WITH FRIENDS INCLUDING FORMER PARSONS CLASSMATES,
DECORATORS EDWARD ZAJAC AND RICHARD CALLAHAN, 1976. OCEAN RIDGE, FIRE ISLAND, SUMMER OF 1962.

suburban spaces outfitted with chinoiserie special effects, urban interiors that reference the Paris of Napoléon Bonaparte or the Rome of Julius Caesar or the Pink City of the maharajahs of Jaipur. "A really good designer should be able to do different things," the designer explains in typically forthright fashion. "If you're talented you can't help being influenced by everything you see—and I've been influenced by a lot of things." Britt's approach to domestic settings is nonetheless his own: extravagant, optimistic, spirited, often outrageously theatrical. Rooms swagger with a startling blend of outsize architectural details, imperially scaled spaces, soaring canopy beds, powerful saturated colors, unrelentingly symmetrical arrangements of furniture and art, full-figured upholstery, and impactful clusters of matching objects.

"To Tom, if two candlesticks look good, twenty look even better," says architectural designer Peter Napolitano, who worked with Britt on some of the decorator's most identifiable interiors. "That sense of drama, that appreciation of scale, is something I've always admired about him. I think he's always had that, right from the beginning."

Back in the late 1950s, the precociously suave Britt and his classmates at New York City's Parsons School of Design—among them the tastemakers-in-waiting Angelo Donghia, Edward Zajac, and Richard Callahan, as well as Julie Creveling, Britt's future wife, who would become a noted photo stylist—were assigned to head out and bring back the one fabric they believed was the most wonderful textile in the city. "They wanted to see what kind of taste and flair you had," Britt recounts today, resting in the polychrome splendor of the Moghul-inspired master bedroom at his weekend house in Water Mill, New York. "Testing the waters, to see who would sink or swim."

Britt sensed that his fellow students would never be brave enough to knock on the door of Rose Cumming's dramatic purple-walled shop in midtown Manhattan. "People were scared to death of her," he says of Cumming, an Australian beauty turned New York millionaire's mistress turned American decorating's eccentric grande dame. Of course, that's precisely where he headed, and next thing Britt knew, "She locked the door and started pulling out beautiful Chinese brocades and robes to show me." A visit that started as a personal dare soon established itself as a meeting of minds. Cumming, like Britt, loved deep, brilliant, even malevolent colors—peacock, jade, sulfur, cerise, and, most important to Britt, aubergine, which is practically his signature—glittering metallics, and earthquaking palettes. She also was captivated by Qing furniture laden with mother-of-pearl, which she kept (to its detriment) year-round in the garden of her brownstone; similar furniture, especially in the form of low tables perfectly sized to support a cocktail or set down a phone, would become an integral part of Britt's own aesthetic.

Echoes of the designer's youth in Kansas City—where Thomas Burgin Britt was born in 1936, the elder son of James Thomas Britt, a prominent lawyer, and his civic-leader wife, Ruth Evangeline Burgin, a clergyman's daughter from San Antonio, Texas—infuse his interiors, too. "There's a lot of style out there and some very sophisticated houses," says the designer, rattling off a litany of names who set the city's singular style, including Lucy Drage and her cataracts of flowered English chintz and Altaire & Crawley, a.k.a. Town and Country Decorations, "a very conservative firm run by Kenneth Crawley and Earl Altaire," an artist who had painted all the furniture at La Fonda, Santa Fe's legendary hotel, back in the 1920s.

Britt's love of black rooms—brooding, unconventional, shrine-like—can be traced back to the late 1940s. "When I was about twelve, my grandfather's second wife, Gigi, let me loose on the third floor of their house, which had been maids' quarters, but since they had no live-in maids, I could do what I wanted," the decorator says. "I painted the walls black and the floors white. On one wall my grandmother had shelves that I concealed behind screens I made with lining paper from Cook's Paint and Varnish. I painted the paper silver and then cut it into big pieces so it looked like big pieces of silver leaf." Britt made extra money by refinishing and selling secondhand metal garden furniture, and at age sixteen he largely redecorated the family house, a project that included painting the sleeping porch dark green after seeing a verdant William Pahlmann room published in *House & Garden*.

"I was always looking at decorating magazines—*House & Garden, House Beautiful*, even *Town & Country*," Britt explains. "I loved looking at the work of Van Day Truex a lot, and when I found out he was originally from Kansas, I was in a state of shock. How did he come from out here? And then I learned that Mrs. Archibald Brown, who founded McMillen, was from St. Louis. I didn't realize that so many of the designers I worshipped weren't native New Yorkers."

Britt's tendency to light rooms with battalions of candles or lanterns, often Moroccan or Indian, references Malang House of Design, a Kansas City florist and party planner whose patio was illumined, he says, "with eighty or a hundred candles with glass chimney shades that were washed with red or pink lacquer." The designer's frequently deployed dense grids of identically framed and matted prints or etchings, typically all from one series, stem from a memory of Peggy Sloan, a red-headed Kansas City society decorator who Britt says was known for "very pretty" pale blue and lilac rooms with French Provincial furniture and a shop where the sky-colored walls were lined with nineteenth-century Napoléonic battle prints.

"It made an impressive statement, and I fell in love with those pictures then and there," Britt says. On a family trip to New Orleans, he continues, "I saw the same ones at Lieutaud, a famous print dealer on Rue Royale, and realized that I could sell those prints to decorators in other cities. Somehow my parents let me buy a bunch of them, get on a train—when I was only a student at Southwest High School—and do just that. Once I arrived in whatever town, I'd open the phone book, look up all the designers, and visit them."

Especially important to Britt's aesthetic development was Frederick Emlyn Fender, a Missouri artist, antiques dealer, and decorator who lived in a scarlet-red Victorian house in Independence, a town about ten miles east of Kansas City. "When I was growing up, I was very starved to find people I could relate to, who shared my whole feeling for design, and Emlyn Fender was very instrumental," Britt explains. "It was amazing what he could do. He carved fabulous looking mirrors in Chinese Chippendale style, but in something like pickled wood, which was divine. He made marbleized paper and covered walls with it. At his house, he painted the walls of the staircase with trompe-l'oeil clothes hanging from pegs. Emlyn had a very offbeat color sense, too, very experimental, like combining raspberry-red and hot pink. My palette is different but it's an echo of Fender's color combinations. His whole viewpoint had a huge impact on me."

While Britt was enrolled in Parsons School of Design in the 1950s, the "five or six months" he spent in Europe as part of the curriculum sparked a wanderlust that has taken him to India, Asia, South America, Europe, and beyond, all of which reverberate throughout his decades of work. "Parsons had real aplomb then," he says, adding that Stanley Barrows, then the director of the school's interior design department, led the tour. "We went through France, Italy, and England, with Stanley, into places not open to the public, so many private homes. It was sensational." Students toured buildings, interiors, and gardens, met architects, designers, and collectors, and sketched architectural details, from the columns at Covent Garden to the doorcases at Versailles.

After graduating from New York University with a bachelor of science in 1959 ("My father wanted me to get a degree from NYU, which I got and which had absolutely zero influence on me"), Britt went in search of a decorating job. "I only wanted to work for Billy Baldwin, whose work was very chaste, classic, and of the moment," he says. "It wasn't in a time warp, and it was very fresh and had an enormous sense of style." Unfortunately, the desired position did not materialize—his classmate Zajac ended up being hired. Instead, Britt spent several years working for John Gerald, a vice president of Manhattan's W & J Sloane department store and a former business partner of British decorator Syrie Maugham.

Not long after Gerald left Sloane in 1963, Britt tried for a position at dealer-decorator Yale Burge, only to realize his services weren't needed, largely because his Parsons classmate Angelo Donghia had become the firm's rising star and its new partner. Shrugging off that setback, Britt simply decided to open his own firm in 1964, first operating from a desk at dealer Frederick

P. Victoria's shop. "I knew some people in New York City, obviously, and I had contacts in Kansas City, all very top families like the Evanses, Paxtons, Browns, and Lightons, a lot of whom lived in the neighborhood I grew up in," he observes. "I quickly got a coterie of clients. They liked the way I decorated, which was more chic and edited than they were used to and a lot more dramatic. Even some of my most conservative clients wanted Hollywood moments. But the acid test is comfort and livability—that and dining rooms should always be fantasies."

Flights of imagination have always been integral to Britt's work for high-flying clients such as the Rajmata of Jaipur, California's Swanson wine dynasty, and the Solomon family that ran Manhattan's Abraham & Straus department stores. Extravagantly tented living rooms straight out of Percier and Fontaine's playbook meet crisply trellised dining rooms that are a mod take on ancien-régime garden pavilions. Eighteenth-century French furniture stands on sassy graphic dhurries custom-made in India. Empire and Regency antiques join smart tortoiseshell-veneer tables produced by Burgin, the short-lived custom-made furniture showroom that Britt launched in the 1970s with Guillermo Piedrahita, a Colombian entrepreneur and Parsons classmate. As American interior design goes, Britt's portfolio is one of decided extravagance and unrepentant glamour. In short, it's fabulous.

CLOCKWISE, FROM UPPER LEFT: THE DESIGNER AT HIS FORTIETH-BIRTHDAY PARTY.
WITH GUILLERMO PIEDRAHITA, THE CO-OWNER OF BURGIN, HIS AND BRITT'S CUSTOM-FURNITURE BUSINESS, 2006.
WALKING IN THE MOROCCAN DESERT, CIRCA 1980. THE DESIGNER'S NEW YORK CITY LIVING ROOM DRESSED
IN BLUE SATIN UPHOLSTERY. BRITT WITH ELIZABETH SWANSON, A FRIEND AND CLIENT, 2004.
GATEWAY INTO THE COURTYARD OF THE BARN HOUSE ON BRITT'S PROPERTY IN WATER MILL, LONG ISLAND.

During my thirty-five-year stewardship of *Architectural Digest*, Tom Britt interiors appeared over sixty times in the magazine's pages. Now, that's impressive. In his first appearance, in the November/December 1974 issue, we described Tom as "greatly talented and greatly eccentric." This description proved true as, year after year, Tom's work beguiled us and kept us on our toes. He designs both spaces that are the perfect backdrop for fine English antiques and ones that are redolent of a crisp modernism. Tom's flexibility is what keeps his interiors so fresh.

Tom knows his design history and deploys references to many periods and styles in the most sophisticated and erudite way. His work is big and bold, or as he would put it, "Everything I do tends to the huge. I don't like fussy things." His strength is in creating unified architectural backgrounds and incorporating contrasting textures, strong infusions of color, and his signature large-scale furnishings.

In the January 2005 issue of *Architectural Digest*, we presented the "Deans of American Design." Tom was on the list of luminaries that we described as "the United States' best architects and interior designers, whose outstanding achievements have propelled them to the top echelons of their fields." Tom certainly fills that bill. His cleanly composed, beautifully scaled rooms feature dramatic accents while eschewing "tricks and trends." I'll never forget seeing my first Britt room, and I can never see enough—whether in person or in pictures.

In my eyes, Tom Britt is the most underrated designer in the world. He's also lots of fun.

Paige Rense Noland
West Palm Beach, Florida

ACKNOWLEDGMENTS

This book could not have happened without the continued support of
Architectural Digest and the many editors who for decades have fostered, celebrated,
and documented the career of Tom Britt.

The following people were integral to the making of this publication:

Julie Britt and Rodrigo Aedo Reyes

Charles Miers, Margaret Russell, Richard Pandiscio, William Loccisano, Peter Napolitano,
Marcelo Cadiz, Wendy Carduner, Paulette Streeval, and Aleksandra Eckhard

Marianne Brown, Allison Ingram, Ivan Shaw, Cynthia Cathcart,
Stan Friedman, and Deirdre McCabe Nolan

PHOTOGRAPHY CREDITS

Jaime Ardiles-Arce: 146–47, 148–49, 151, 152–53, 154, 246–47, 280–81, 282–83, 285, 300

Jaime Ardiles-Arce/*Architectural Digest*, October 1980 © Condé Nast: 78–79, 81, 82–83, 84–85, 86–87

Jaime Ardiles-Arce/*Architectural Digest*, November 1985 © Condé Nast: 6, 235, 236–37, 238–39, 241, 242–43, 245

Jaime Ardiles-Arce/*Architectural Digest*, September 1986 © Condé Nast: 88–89

Jaime Ardiles-Arce/*Architectural Digest*, February 1988 © Condé Nast: 198–99, 200–1, 202, 204–5

Jaime Ardiles-Arce/*Architectural Digest*, July 1990 © Condé Nast: 46, 48–49, 50–51, 52–53, 54–55

Jaime Ardiles-Arce/*Architectural Digest*, November 1990 © Condé Nast: 5, 124–25, 126–27, 128–29, 130–31

Jaime Ardiles-Arce/*Architectural Digest*, April 1991 © Condé Nast: 20–21, 22–23, 24–25, 26–27

Jaime Ardiles-Arce/*Architectural Digest*, August 1991 © Condé Nast: 277, 288–89, 290–91

Jaime Ardiles-Arce/*Architectural Digest*, May 1992 © Condé Nast: 112, 114–15, 116–17, 119, 120–21

Jaime Ardiles-Arce/*Architectural Digest*, August 1992 © Condé Nast: 166–67, 169, 170, 171, 173, 174–75

Jaime Ardiles-Arce/*Architectural Digest*, November 1992 © Condé Nast: 138–39, 140–41, 143, 144–45

Jaime Ardiles-Arce/*Architectural Digest*, May 1993 © Condé Nast: 132–33, 135, 136–37

Richard Champion/*Architectural Digest*, July–August 1976 © Condé Nast: 90–91, 92–93, 94–95, 96–97

Roger Davies: 58–59, 60–61, 62–63, 64–65

Jonathan DeCola: 292, 299 (individual photographs courtesy of Tom Britt)

Phillip Ennis: 206–7

Scott Frances/*Architectural Digest*, November 2001 © Condé Nast: 176, 178–79, 180–81, 182–83

Scott Frances/*Architectural Digest*, March 2003 © Condé Nast: 208–9, 210–11, 212–13, 214–15, 217

Scott Frances/*Architectural Digest*, February 2004 © Condé Nast: 56, 123

Scott Frances/*Architectural Digest*, February 2007 © Condé Nast: 11, 12–13, 14–15, 16–17, 18–19

Scott Frances/*Architectural Digest*, April 2008 © Condé Nast: 67, 68, 70–71, 72–73, 75, 76–77

Jeff Hirsch/New York Social Diary: 2

Max Kim-Bee: 248–49, 250, 253, 254, 255, 256–57, 259, 260–61, 262–63, 264–65, 267, 268–69, 270–71, 273, 274–75, 278–79, 286–87

Joshua McHugh: 36–37, 38, 40–41, 42–43, 44–45

Mary E. Nichols/*Architectural Digest*, August 1985 © Condé Nast: 218–19, 220–21, 222–23, 225

Durston Saylor/*Architectural Digest*, February 1999 © Condé Nast: 185, 186, 188–89, 191, 192, 194–95

Tony Soluri/*Architectural Digest*, July 2010 © Condé Nast: 226–27, 228–29, 230–31, 232–33

Robert Thien/*Architectural Digest*, February 1995 © Condé Nast: 156–57, 158–59, 160–61, 162–63, 165

Simon Upton/The Interior Archive: 196–97

Peter Vitale/*Architectural Digest*, September 1979 © Condé Nast: 104–5, 106–7, 108–9, 110–11

Peter Vitale/*Architectural Digest*, April 1982 © Condé Nast: 28–29, 30–31, 32–33, 34–35

Peter Vitale/*Architectural Digest*, August 1982 © Condé Nast: 98–99, 100–1, 102–3

FIRST PUBLISHED IN THE UNITED STATES OF AMERICA IN 2017
BY RIZZOLI INTERNATIONAL PUBLICATIONS, INC.
300 PARK AVENUE SOUTH
NEW YORK, NY 10010
WWW.RIZZOLIUSA.COM

COPYRIGHT © 2017 BY RIZZOLI INTERNATIONAL PUBLICATIONS, INC.
TEXT COPYRIGHT © 2017 BY MITCHELL OWENS
ISBN: 978-0-8478-6031-9
LIBRARY OF CONGRESS CONTROL NUMBER: 2017937209

PHILIP REESER, EDITOR
ALYN EVANS, PRODUCTION MANAGER
MEGAN CONWAY, COPY EDITOR

RICHARD PANDISCIO, CREATIVE DIRECTOR
WILLIAM LOCCISANO, DESIGNER

2017 2018 2019 2020 / 10 9 8 7 6 5 4 3 2 1

PRINTED AND BOUND IN CHINA